T0146846

THE PRACTICAL STRATEGIES SERIES
IN GIFTED EDUCATION

series editors
FRANCES A. KARNES & KRISTEN R. STEPHENS

Arts Education for Gifted Learners

Jesse Rachel Cukierkorn, Ph.D.

Routledge
Taylor & Francis Group

NEW YORK AND LONDON

First published 2008 by Prufrock Press Inc.

Published 2021 by Routledge
605 Third Avenue, New York, NY 10017
2 Park Square, Milton Park, Abingdon, Oxon OX14 4RN

Routledge is an imprint of the Taylor & Francis Group, an informa business

ISBN 13: 978-1-59363-319-6 (pbk)

Contents

The Practical Strategies Series in Gifted Education offers teachers, counselors, administrators, parents, and other interested parties up-to-date instructional techniques and information on a variety of issues pertinent to the field of gifted education. Each guide addresses a focused topic and is written by an individual with authority on the issue. Several guides have been published. Among the titles are:

- *Acceleration Strategies for Teaching Gifted Learners*
- *Curriculum Compacting: An Easy Start to Differentiating for High-Potential Students*
- *Enrichment Opportunities for Gifted Learners*
- *Independent Study for Gifted Learners*
- *Motivating Gifted Learners*
- *Questioning Strategies for Teaching the Gifted*
- *Social & Emotional Teaching Strategies*
- *Using Media & Technology With Gifted Students*

For a current listing of available guides within the series, please contact Prufrock Press at (800) 998-2208 or visit http://www.prufrock.com.

Introduction

How is talent defined in a young artist? What is the role of art education in gifted education? How much value is placed on the arts in school and at home? These questions face many parents and educators, especially when a child shows a great affinity for making art, music, or dance and is interested in improving his or her abilities in these areas. Current beliefs and values about art and art education guide parents and teachers as they nurture a child who is talented in the visual or performing arts. Confidence in art, as a critical and complex experience, is the first step in supporting the artistically talented student. Over time, there are several different ways in which teachers and parents can follow through, maintain, and support an artistically talented child.

The general goals of this volume are to increase awareness of artistic expression, reveal the characteristics of artistically talented students, describe program options, and share an approach for supporting the affective needs of these students. Compared to other countries, the United States has very little support for the arts in education and in society. Rare gifts and talents often are untapped and untaught, with just a portion of the population with artistic talent being served. Furthermore, there still is much to be learned in terms of understanding these students' abilities and needs. Talented individuals have the potential to make terrific contributions to the art and culture of society. Practical strategies and resources are needed to foster artistic expression and to ensure that artists can excel in their respective fields.

Many children enjoy participating in the arts and excel in these activities. However, it is very difficult for educators and parents to gauge achievement in the arts unlike achievements in academic and intellectual pursuits. While the twofold term "gifted and talented" often is used in education and in the Javits Act (1988), many states distinguish giftedness from talent in their regulations for serving youth by defining separate categories for intellectually gifted and artistically talented. Gagné (2003) distinguished giftedness from talent more clearly. In his model, giftedness means the possession and use of untrained and spontaneously expressed natural abilities (called aptitudes or gifts) in at least one domain to a degree that places a child among the top 10% of his or her age peers. In contrast, talent designates the superior mastery of systematically developed abilities or skills and knowledge in at least one area of endeavor to a degree that places the child among the top 10% of his or her age peers who are active in that field (Gagné, 2003). The following section provides profiles of four young artists, all of whom attend programs with extensive admission criteria and who have demonstrated advanced achievement by winning top awards or scholarships within their school or program. From these profiles and others, it becomes evident that setting high expectations for achievement in the arts and making contact with other artists are powerful components of talent development.

Tobias—Musical Theatre (17 Years Old)

Tobias has stood out from his peers for his creative abilities in dancing and singing since he was in the second grade. In elementary school, he received encouragement from enthusiastic teachers who emphasized lessons in creative movement. Tobias admitted that, at first, he was not always serious about his abilities. He initially danced, sang, and performed in musical theatre due to the accolades that he received and because people said that he was really good at it. Only later did one of his instructors at the arts conservatory teach him to have faith in his own abilities and ownership of the "drive to perform." This instructor taught Tobias that each and every time he is performing he has to "tell the story" whether he is acting, singing, or dancing. At 17, Tobias feels that he is now a completely different person, because he has the passion for performance.

Tobias's mother lets him focus on the things that he loves. Although he has a B average in high school, she is not overly concerned about his grades. Tobias feels that his mother's willingness to let him focus on his creative abilities has contributed greatly to the development of his talent.

Ashlee—Creative Writing (14 Years Old)

At the age of 13, Ashlee began attending a cluster arts magnet program without any previous training in writing. In the sixth grade, one of her teachers read several of her short stories, recognized her potential, and recommended that she audition for the program. Although the audition process intimidated her, she was excited to learn that there was such a place for her to be creative.

Ashlee sees the depressing environment of her low-income neighborhood as a negative motivator. She says that it drives her to be even better because she doesn't want to be like the people around her in the neighborhood. Once she is alone, in her own room, she can block out all of the negative influences of the neighborhood by putting on music and writing while she sits on her bed. In contrast, Ashlee feels inspired when she leaves her home high school to attend the cluster arts magnet school. She feels that the environment, both school and neighborhood, is safer. The other students are open for discussions and are really welcoming. There aren't as many cliques as compared to her home school, and she doesn't feel as inhibited because there is less fear about what others might say about her writing.

Shara—Visual Art (11 Years Old)

At 5 years old, Shara started taking art lessons from an artist living in her neighborhood. She always liked a variety of visual art forms, and experimented with different kinds of painting, drawing, ceramics, and crafts. Several members of Shara's family, as well as some of her friends, support her art endeavors. Her older brother, Scott, also an artist, introduced her to Manga, which is the Japanese style of art print comics and cartoons. Shara's father lets her use the scanner at his medical lab and then Shara uses Adobe Photoshop to create her own digital comic series. Shara's digital imagery exists only on the Web where she shares them with friends at school and those that she has met online. She does not publish her cartoons in print.

Shara attends an elementary magnet school for the arts that also serves talented secondary students after school. It is here that Shara met Liz, an older student, who is now teaching her how to knit and crochet. Shara feels that Liz is very compatible and understanding. Liz explains the craft techniques in detail and has shown Shara how to incorporate several of her Manga designs into art class assignments. When Shara doesn't understand something, Liz always tries to explain the steps in a simpler way. Shara feels that Liz has made a difference in helping her develop her talent because she is on a similar journey—trying to find herself as an artist. Shara says that Liz has taught her to feel that "art is my teacher."

Lamar—Classical Piano (16 Years Old)

Lamar has been playing piano since he was 6 or 7 years old. When he was little, he used to go next door to his grandmother's house to play the piano. He wanted to take lessons like his older cousin, and eventually his family relented and Lamar was able to start studying. He has had several different teachers throughout his training. Along the way, Lamar feels that some of the instructors were better than others. In his opinion, the teachers who contributed most to his talent development taught him fundamentals about playing music and demonstrated that they wanted the best for all of their students, not just one or two of them. The instructors who he felt did not contribute to his development allowed him to settle for less, but he did not let them hold him back. Lamar feels that the time he may have lost in developing his talent was spent "just growing up" and becoming more mature. Lamar now attends a music conservatory. At the conservatory he has learned to evaluate himself on a day-to-day basis. He also met a good friend at the conservatory, a young percussionist, who taught him to listen more closely to certain aspects of the music. In his free time, Lamar gets inspiration and relaxation from riding his bicycle along the riverfront while listening to all types of music on his digital audio player.

Understanding the Purpose of the Arts

Raising the levels of arts awareness is an important initial goal. The differences between terms such as *art*, *the arts*, and *fine arts* are easily misunderstood. The arts, a term used throughout this book, applies both to the fine and applied arts. In the fine arts, work is structured around the discovery of problem situations. The fine artist must create his or her own problem, as well as the solution (Getzels & Csikszentmihalyi, 1976). The fine arts refer to painting, drawing, sculpture, printmaking, media arts, literature, theatre, music, and dance. Art or visual art refers only to the first five of these. The performing arts include dance, vocal and instrumental music, musical theatre, and theatre design. Furthermore, it is important to note the difference between fine arts and applied arts such as architecture, interior design, jewelry making, textile design, and graphics. Aesthetic concerns are significant to the applied arts; however, the work of applied artists is concerned with presented problems, such as making objects with functional purposes. As an educator, parent, or student talented in the arts, one must promote arts awareness. Understanding the purpose of art in our society is a critical step in supporting artistic talent.

The Power of the Arts

The current state of arts education advocacy has fueled a fascination with the effects of music or art education on learning in other subjects. Some art educators feel that in order for arts education to be valued, carry-over effects into other subjects must be explored. Rather than focus on achievement in other subjects, energy would be better spent looking into what the arts have to offer that nothing else can teach. Participating in the arts, and engaging in the processes of making visual art, music, dance, and theatre are critical and complex experiences. Although there are few empirical studies validating the existence of cognitive processes inherent in the arts, a significant investigation of the cognitive outcomes of arts education is underway at Harvard University (Winner & Hetland, 2000). To complement these findings, the inherent benefits of arts education are presented here.

Haroutounian (1995) outlined four perceptual and cognitive processes that are inherent in the arts: perceptual discrimination, metaperception, creative interpretation, and the dynamic of performance. Perceptual discrimination begins with fine-tuned sensory awareness. According to Haroutounian, visual and performing artists view, hear, and sense the world with acuity and a special awareness. For example, she stated that young talented musicians could discriminate subtle rhythm patterns, melodic shapes, and the tonal color of different sounds; and young talented actors are highly attuned to interactions with fellow actors and the audience. Haroutounian defined metaperception as the artistic parallel to *metacognition*, a term used to describe mental monitoring in cognitive thinking. Metaperception also has been referred to as artistic knowing, thinking with an aesthetic sense, qualitative responsiveness, or qualitative intelligence. Metaperception can be understood as the internal manipulation and monitoring of the acute senses, perceptions, and emotions. Haroutounian described the artistic interpretive process as becoming more creative the further a student reworks and refines his or her art or performance. The end result is a unique personalized statement or creative interpretation. Finally, Haroutounian recognized that visual and performing artists do not create their work in a vacuum. The dynamic of performance refers to the special abilities developed in the process of communicating a work of art. Haroutounian acknowledged that art is an aesthetic experience shared between the audience and the visual and performing artist. For example, as an actor becomes more aware of what the audience perceives, the audience more closely connects with the actor's interpretation of the work.

Other authors have studied the processes that are inherent in the arts. According to Milbrath (1998), children who are talented in visual art actually see the world differently. She claimed that artists encode visual information more accurately, and see the world less in terms of concepts and more in terms of shapes and visual surface features. Milbrath noted that when typical children draw pictures, they are guided more by an effort to communicate their understanding of the objects they are trying to draw and less by the actual visual properties of our world. Because they can override what they know about objects and remain faithful to the depiction of what they see, talented young artists are able to draw more realistically. Rostan (2003) found that in making their drawings and paintings, highly motivated 6- and 7-year-old artists search for more effective techniques. In addition, the efforts of these talented young artists require unique cognitive abilities such as planning and monitoring ongoing activity, learning from past experience and from other models, persisting, and evaluating one's own work. These are not just characteristics commonly associated with visually artistic students, but point to special cognitive abilities and a unique way of sensing the world and solving problems.

Winner and Hetland (2000) conducted the first and only to-date comprehensive and quantitative study of research that has investigated the academic or cognitive outcomes of arts education. They first searched for all studies from 1950–1999 (published and unpublished, appearing in English) that tested the claim that studying the arts leads to some form of academic improvement. The searches turned up 11,467 articles, books, theses, conference presentations, technical reports, unpublished papers, and unpublished data (Winner & Hetland, 2000). Once the irrelevant reports and program descriptions lacking an empirical test were removed, 188 reports investigating the relationship between one or more arts areas to one or more academic areas remained. The authors calculated a total of 275 effect size *rs* and then conducted 10 meta-analyses. Clear causal links were demonstrated in three areas: listening to music and spatial-temporal reasoning, learning to play music and spatial reasoning, and classroom drama and verbal skills.

In 26 reports (36 effect sizes), a medium-sized causal relationship was found between listening to music and improvement in spatial-temporal reasoning (Winner & Hetland, 2000). Winner and Hetland found this interesting because of the possible suggestion that music and spatial reasoning are related psychologically and/or neurologically. The authors also suggested that further research is needed to understand the mechanism by which certain types of music influence spatial skills. A large causal relationship was found between learning to make music and spatial-temporal reasoning based on 19 reports (29 effect sizes). The authors found a large effect even when students did not learn to read standard music notation.

Based on 80 reports (107 effect sizes), a medium-sized causal link was found between enacting texts in a drama classroom and a variety of verbal areas (Winner & Hetland, 2000). In all of the cases studied, students who enacted texts were compared to students who read the same texts but did not enact them. Some of the verbal skills that improved were oral understanding (recall of stories), reading readiness, reading achievement, oral language, writing, written understanding (recall of stories), and vocabulary. The drama experiences helped the students' verbal skills with respect to the texts enacted as well as new, nonenacted texts.

Whether or not the argument for carry-over effects into other subjects is compelling, the inherent power of the arts is only as critical and complex as one makes it. Figure 1 offers suggestions for teachers, parents, and students who are talented in the arts or who have a special awareness of their abilities in this area that they would like to develop.

Teacher Strategies

- Particularly for the gifted educator or practicing artist, it is important to share your own experiences with creative work and the role that meta-cognition and/or metaperception have played in the artistic process.
- When sharing your own work, explain the formal problems that interest you and direct students to other artists who are interested in the same problems in your discipline.

Parent Strategies

- When you answer children's questions about the arts with patience and good humor, you are communicating to them that their interests are valid and important. Even if you do not know the answer, use children's questions and expressions of interest as guides into further learning and explorations of music, dance, theatre, or visual art.
- Help children develop artistic growth and encourage mental growth in their area of interest.
- Teach children how to budget time, organize materials, store completed work, and improve work habits.

Student Strategies

- Seek to discover what kinds of formal problems other artists try to solve, either by reading about famous work or directly questioning the artists that you meet. The more that you are aware of the formal problems that are unique to your discipline, the easier it will be to find the ones that interest you the most.
- Even when you are creating an artistic piece or practicing your art for your own enjoyment, try to use planning and problem-solving skills in your approach.
- Keep a journal of your artistic reflections. As you practice or work on a particular creative piece, try to record your experiences with metaperception. If you save these notes in a journal or inside of your sketchbook, you will be able to return to your writings and learn from past experiences. Later, you will be able to expand upon these writings and possibly use a description of your metaperception or problem-solving strategies in your college entrance essays.

Figure 1. Practical strategies for unleashing the power of the arts.

Characteristics of Artistically Talented Students

Because so few researchers and educators have studied the incidence of high ability in the arts, there is little agreement about what constitutes art talent, what it looks like, and how it should be defined (Clark & Zimmerman, 1998; Zimmerman, 2004). Clark and Zimmerman (1998) state that this lack of agreement may be because identifying talent in the arts is complex and requires more than one indicator. Young artists usually are recognized for their outstanding achievements in visual art, drama, dance, or music, yet behind those achievements lay certain characteristics and skills that point to potential and trace the development of talent in the arts. Although only a few major empirical studies have sought to identify the cognitive and personality characteristics of students talented in the visual and performing arts, some of these same studies have shaped our understanding of talent development and creative work. For a summary of the characteristics of artistic children, see Appendix A.

Visual Artists

Perhaps the most famous study regarding young visual art-ists was conducted by Getzels and Csikszentmihalyi (1976). In 1963, these researchers gathered information from students at the School of the Art Institute of Chicago. The art students in this study were given open-ended drawing assignments of a still life. Getzels and Csikszentmihalyi observed the artistic process of the students and from these observations a model of creativity based on problem finding was developed. The authors described the visual art students as highly unconventional, socially aloof, radical, sensitive, imaginative, and naïve in comparison with non-art students. They also found that those who kept problems open longer produced more creative solutions, and art students who had engaged in problem-finding activities proved to have greater success in the profession even years later.

Revisiting the biographical data of successful artists, Getzels and Csikszentmihalyi (1976) were able to describe some of the common attributes found in the artists' accounts of early child-hood. Like other children, the young visual artists drew cartoon characters, copied drawings of comic-book heroes, and made caricatures of classmates. The artists claimed that although they did not feel their drawings were substantially better than their same-age peers, their drawings received more notice and praise. They recalled making drawings to amuse other classmates in ele-mentary school and often were asked to design and build things for their elementary school teachers. Compared to their class-mates, these young future artists devoted most of their energy to drawing.

A majority of the sculptors in Bloom's (1985) study liked to draw as children, yet did not have parents or relatives who were artists or who worked on art projects with them. As children, these subjects' early attempts at making art were purposeful, intending to represent a subject accurately as opposed to scrib-bling, doodling, or coloring in coloring books. They practiced sketching pets, and copied pictures from books of animals and cartoon characters. One sculptor, at the age of 5, was permitted to use a jackknife so that he could carve things. In elementary school, the sculptors produced a lot of artwork and constructions, doing so in their free time and even sometimes in school when they were supposed to be engaged in something else. They built objects to resemble things they saw, such as a castle in a book, as well as things that were functional, like a birdhouse. Bloom noted that the parents saved a considerable amount of the children's earliest artwork, yet gave little direction to their children as far as pursuing a career. Although some of the young artists were praised for their drawings, the children were not guided to quality teachers nor were their efforts recognized as latent talents waiting to develop (Bloom, 1985). Nevertheless, Bloom concluded that none of his subjects reached their levels of expertise without a supportive and encouraging environment and a long and intensive period of training, first from loving and warm teachers, and then from demanding and rigorous master teachers.

Based on their review of the research regarding artistically talented students, Clark and Zimmerman (2004) stated that well-developed drawing skills, high cognitive abilities, affective intensity, interest, and motivation are the core characteristics of young visual artists. Some would argue that talented visual artists must demonstrate both advanced skills and innovation (Clark & Zimmerman, 2004). Other indicators of talent in the arts may be high levels of motivation, passion, perseverance, or problem-solving skills (Clark & Zimmerman, 1998). However, the authors noted that these traits may or may not be present at the same levels in any student at any given time.

Bloom (1985) contended that talent in the arts might emerge at different ages and different grade levels. A common characteristic of talented students in visual art is they produce a large volume of work over a sustained period of time (Clark & Zimmerman, 2004; Golomb, 1995; Milbrath, 1998). Most authors agree that well-developed drawing ability is a core characteristic of young talented artists (Clark & Zimmerman, 2004; Golomb, 1995; Milbrath, 1998; Winner, 1996); therefore, precocious drawing ability is the focus of studies that illuminate the emergence of visual art talent.

According to Winner (1996), there is conflicting evidence about whether visually artistic children demonstrate advanced compositional strategies. However, Golomb (1995) stated that artistically talented children are more likely to organize their drawings according to the principle of asymmetrical balance, whereas typical children are more likely to use symmetrical balance.

Milbrath's (1998) longitudinal and cross-sectional studies of talented children in visual art are an important contribution to the field because they represent the first systematic, large-scale, and theoretically grounded studies of talented young visual artists. All of the talented students in Milbrath's studies exclusively used lines to stand for the edges of things, even in their earliest drawings (age 3 to 6). This is in contrast to less talented visual artists who frequently used active lines to stand as forms (up until the age of 10). An example of an active line is the way that a single line stands for a limb in the typical representation of a human. Therefore, Milbrath noted that a clear sign of artistic talent is the ability to use a line to stand for an "edge," in contrast to typical children who use a line to stand for a "thing."

Because artistically talented children see the world in terms of its edge and surface features, they are able to make view-specific drawings long before other children (Milbrath, 1998). By the age of 7, the talented art students in both of Milbrath's studies had drawn human figures in unusual positions such as three-quarter views of faces, back views, and profiles, as well as figures distorted and foreshortened by perspective. The ability to draw realistically also means that talented children draw the human figure with correct proportions.

Performing Artists

Benjamin Bloom's (1985) interviews with talented individuals and their parents contributed much to our understanding of the characteristics of talented students in the performing arts. As children, the musicians in his study were described as quick to learn the piano, and both their parents and teachers recognized their special abilities. Music was present to some degree in all of their homes, and a large percentage of the musicians began taking lessons before the age of 6. Shuter-Dyson (1985) noted that musical talent can reveal itself as young as 1 or 2 years of age, which is earlier than in any other talent domain. Sosniak (1985), one of Bloom's researchers, also stated that one of the early signs of talent in music is a strong interest and pleasure in musical sounds. Furthermore, Shuter-Dyson (1985) indicated that the core of musical aptitude is assumed to be the ability to detect pitch, duration of pitch, and rhythm.

Bloom's (1985) study often is understood as evidence that eminent artists start out as ordinary children but have dedicated parents and teachers motivating them to cultivate their talent (Winner, 1996). Signs of unusual ability were clearly evident in Bloom's subjects. Musicians were quick to learn the piano, and sculptors recalled drawing constantly. Most of the interviewees said they learned easily in their chosen domain but did not learn as quickly in other content areas at school.

Bloom's (1985) study was influential in that it distinguished three stages in the career of the talented individual. In the *early years* (the first stage), the individual is attracted to the talent domain. In the *middle years* (the second stage), the individual becomes committed to the domain, and finally, during the *adult years* (the third stage), the individual makes the domain the center of his or her life.

Csikszentmihalyi, Rathunde, and Whalen (1993) studied talented young musicians, artists, mathematicians, scientists, and athletes. They found that all of the talented teenagers in their study had personality traits conducive to concentration and endurance, as well as being open to experience. These teenagers were shown to be atypical socially and emotionally in a number of respects; they were highly driven, nonconforming, and independent thinkers. As a group, these students were more conservative in their sexual attitudes and aware of the conflict between productive work and peer relations. The talented students said they gained stimulation from themselves more so than from others and they reported liking solitude far more than most other people. Although it is difficult for these atypical children to find like-minded peers, the talented adolescents also reported a preference to be with others rather than alone. Therefore, although these students felt they gained more from solitude, they still yearned for peer contact. Families of these talented teenagers provided both support and challenge. The students who excelled in this study felt they had achieved a balance between long-term and short-term goals, finding many kinds of rewards in the work they did. The successful young artists showed some of the same qualities that typified young scientists and vice versa.

In another study, Ericsson, Krampe, and Tesch-Romer (1993) found that levels of achievement in piano, violin, ballet, chess, bridge, and athletics were strongly associated with the sheer number of hours spent in practice. In this work, the authors presented a theoretical framework for expert performance, explaining it as the end result of prolonged periods of deliberate practice. They found that the best musicians had practiced twice as many hours as those who were less successful.

Sloboda (1996) conducted a similar study of young musicians in the United Kingdom and found those students who earned the highest achievement grades in their particular musical instrument had practiced 800% more than the students in the lowest ability group. Ericsson et al. (1993) noted that in music and ballet, the higher the level of attained performance, the earlier the age of first exposure to the domain, as well as the age of starting deliberate practice. The authors also extended their theory to elite performers in ballet and pointed to studies regarding the anatomical characteristics of ballet dancers. Ericsson et al. explained that success in a ballet career is dependent upon physical flexibility of the joints, which only can be gained through extensive training before dancers reach the age of 11. Without extensive training at young ages, dancers simply are not physically able to achieve certain ballet positions. In reference to this study, Winner (1996) noted hard work and innate ability are probably confounded. Children who are interested in a particular activity are most likely to be the ones who begin to work at that activity at an early age and who work hardest at it.

One of the differences between musical talent development and visual arts talent development is the age at which extraordinary talent tends to manifest itself (Zimmerman, 2004). Prodigious behavior is evident in music but there have been fewer prodigies in visual art. Seashore (as cited in Shuter-Dyson, 1985) confirmed that basic music qualities are displayed at an early age and reliable measurement of musical talent can be made by age 9 or 10.

Winner (1996) felt that children who are talented in visual art learn differently in that they need far less adult support to learn in their domain than the typical child. Winner defined the term "rage to master" as the powerful drive that talented students have to focus and make sense of their domain. This term also is applied to Winner's case studies of musically talented children. According to her research, musically talented children show sensitivity to the structure of music such as tonality, key, harmony, and rhythm, and they are able to hear the expressive properties of music. Winner explained that this sensitivity to structure is what allows the child to remember music; to play it back easily, either vocally or with an instrument; and to transpose, improvise, and compose new pieces.

Surprisingly, most of the evidence regarding the characteristics and skills of talented students in the performing arts is anecdotal and lacks a theoretical context for the findings. As an example, Gray & Kunkel (2001) stated that the literature regarding talented young dancers is largely a collection of disconnected, quantitatively based perspectives on selected characteristics or behaviors of dancers. Piirto (1992) stated that the development of creativity and talent in actors and dancers is similar to that of musicians and visual artists. Young actors are observant and use what they have observed in the characters they create. She claimed that, from an early age, dancers are interested in movement, and often play games of balance and technique.

Although a few efforts exist to recognize students who have shown an outstanding ability in the arts, such as the National Art Honor Society sponsored by the National Art Education Association (NAEA), and the International Thespian Society sponsored by the Educational Theatre Association (EdTA), very little research attention is given to understanding the characteristics of this population. Most professional organizations in the arts devote their research energy to advocating the position that instruction in the arts contributes to education at all levels and for all children. Although arts education initiatives are important in today's social and economic climate, little energy is left, it seems, to advocate for the exceptionally talented students in their own midst. The organizations that promote and publish most of the research in arts education (NAEA, the Music Educators National Conference [MENC], and EdTA) express concern for children with different learning abilities, yet they do not include in their mission statements or published research agendas any priority for understanding or advancing the education of exceptionally talented students. The National Association for Gifted Children (NAGC) defined a gifted person as "someone who shows, or has the potential for showing, an exceptional level of performance in one or more areas of expression" (2005b, ¶4). The arts division of NAGC specifically "promotes the recognition and acceptance of the visual and performing arts as an essential area of giftedness [and] encourages research in the area of the artistically gifted and talented" (2005a, ¶1). Nevertheless, there is a paucity of research in the area of talented students in the visual and performing arts (Zimmerman, 2004).

Several theorists suggest that development occurs within a specific domain when one is allowed to work intensely within the domain over a long period (Feldman, 1999; Gagné, 2003). When an individual is involved in his or her own growth, more and more effort is devoted to learning and practicing that activity. When talent is just emerging, such as is the case with young artists, commitment must be at an increasing level so that abilities can be taught, refined, and practiced (Coleman, 2002). Tannenbaum (2003) and Gagné (2003) have argued that being in the right place at the right time (the element of chance) is just as important for talent development. Coleman (2002) stated that knowledge, task commitment, networking, and modeling are only acquired in a special setting. Once one has acknowledged the significance and purpose of the arts in our society, focus then can be given to supporting artistically talented children by finding special opportunities for them to observe, create, reflect, and learn.

School programs that focus on the arts are a growing trend in educational improvement. There are approximately 500 public and private elementary, middle, and high schools with a focus on arts education in the United States, and it is estimated that this figure may easily double (Daniel, 2000; Garrick, 2005; Mickelson, 2003). Despite the fact that few states have developed and adopted statewide arts assessments, authors have found that arts students' attitudes toward school and academic achievement are evident in higher scores on standardized academic achievement tests when compared to students in other schools (Elliot, 1999; Wilson, 2001). Wilson (2001) reported arts magnet students find a high degree of satisfaction in their schools:

> They enjoy working closely with their arts teachers, who are models and mentors and often good friends. They value these close relationships with adults who possess skills and knowledge that they themselves wish to acquire. Students also appreciate adults who value them as individuals as well as artistically talented students. (p. 383)

Many visual and performing arts high schools provide pre-professional training for careers in visual art, instrumental music, dance, theatre, technical theatre, creative writing, and voice. Several schools also have developed innovative academic programs relating the arts to other school subjects (Daniel, 2000; Wilson, 2001).

Schools for the visual and performing arts serve several purposes. They provide professional training and serve as an alternative to traditional schools. In these special schools, students benefit from being surrounded by other talented individuals who also are struggling to reach greatness. Although anecdotal, the description of students who are recognized for their talents in the visual and performing arts and accepted into special arts programs is highly appropriate to this discussion. Secondary students who attend magnet schools for the visual and performing arts are noted for their professional aspirations (Wilson, 2001). One can surmise that these students are seriously interested in an environment where they can concentrate on experimenting and working on domain-specific problems (Gratto, 2002; Winner, 1996). Clark and Zimmerman (2004) noted, "One of the most salient characteristics of both academically and artistically talented students is their intense interest and dedication to a specific subject matter and their own desire to develop knowledge, skills, and understanding that lead to self-improvement" (p. 165). Students talented in the arts may stay after school or attend school on Saturdays to rehearse a play, practice for a concert, or complete a portfolio. Programs for the visual and performing arts also may act like a magnet because they draw in students from a diverse area. A variety of program options exist including magnet schools, charter schools, arts centers, and private institutions (Gratto, 2002; Mickelson, 2003). In this section, three different state-supported program options will be explored: cluster arts magnet schools, elementary arts magnet schools, and residential arts schools. Private institutions and the choice to seek private instruction will also be discussed.

Magnet Schools

Magnet schools for the arts primarily emerged in response to the 1970s desegregation crisis in public schools (Rossell, 2005). Early magnet schools offered a peaceful alternative to forced busing, drawing White students to traditionally Black community schools with innovative curriculum and specially focused programs as a means of integrating an entire school district. Magnet schools for the arts remain a popular trend in school choice. Arts magnet schools are characterized by close relationships with the local arts communities (Daniel, 2000; Gratto, 2002; Wilson, 2001), and some schools were even founded by the efforts of local artists and supporters of the arts within the community (Gratto, 2002).

Part of the appeal of these schools is the opportunity they provide in developing potential talent. They are more likely to nurture latent gifts in children because they accommodate different learning styles and capabilities (Daniel, 2000). In fact, one of the characteristics that Wilson (2001) identifies as common to all arts magnet schools is that of a clear integrated arts mission. Although these schools are organized around the study of visual art, graphic design, and performing arts, the mission of arts magnet schools "always extend(s) beyond the arts" (p. 376). Therefore, collaboration between the visual and performing arts and in-depth study of the arts often is integrated with humanities, language arts, and the sciences (Daniel, 2000; Wilson, 2001).

Magnet schools vary greatly in terms of the procedures used for entrance and continued enrollment. Most of the magnet schools that are profiled here use a highly selective process; however some schools only use a lottery system. Although the lotteries usually are blind to race and ethnicity, preference in the lottery may be given for a sibling who wishes to attend a school that his or her brother or sister is already attending. As there are no standardized art tests generally recommended for the identification of students talented in the visual and performing arts (Clark & Zimmerman, 2002), selective schools for the arts rely upon multifactored and multileveled processes.

Whether at the elementary or secondary level, a sampling or portfolio of the child's interest or ability in one of the visual or performing arts usually is required. For example, the portfolio for entrance to the Baton Rouge Center for Visual and Performing Arts may include drawings; a video of the child performing music, drama, or dance; musical compositions; or writing samples (Baton Rouge Center for Visual and Performing Arts, n.d.). If applying for kindergarten, a letter of recommendation may be required. The screening process for a preprofessional program or residential program for the arts also may include a drawing test, demonstration of skills in sight reading music, writing exercise, participation in a dance class, audition of a prepared piece, or an interview. Students typically are required to perform "cold." For example, vocal artists are quickly taught a new piece of music and asked to perform it immediately, so the faculty can determine the student's skill level and potential. Keep in mind that the more selective the entrance process, the more likely the program is to provide the opportunity to develop potential talent.

Cluster Arts Magnet Programs

The Cluster Arts Magnet Program (CAMP) model is just one way in which artistically talented high school students are being served in the United States. Cluster Arts Magnet Programs are public schools that draw talented students in the arts from a surrounding district or county. CAMP schools offer preprofessional arts training with an affiliated academic program, which means students take arts classes onsite for half of the day but attend other academic classes at their home high school. Although the acronym may be misleading, these schools operate year-round and offer credit toward high school graduation (Izawa-Hayden, 2002). According to Dr. Roy S. Fluhrer, current president of the International NETWORK of Schools for the Advancement of Arts Education (NETWORK) and director of the Fine Arts Center (FAC) in Greenville, SC, the CAMP model was named and given the acronym by the NETWORK, in order to distinguish it from other magnet schools and high schools for the visual and performing arts that provide a full-day college preparatory program (personal communication, March 16, 2006). According to the NETWORK, only six exemplary programs exist in the United States, making it a unique, yet highly attractive model (International NETWORK of Schools for the Advancement of Arts Education, n.d.).

Admission to CAMP schools is by audition (Rafferty, 2004). Most schools use transcripts, teacher recommendations, and essays as a screening process, inviting a selection of promising students for an onsite audition. Depending on the discipline, the audition may consist of a portfolio evaluation, a rehearsed monologue, a still-life drawing assignment, or a personal interview with the student. Furthermore, at some CAMP schools, students must audition each year to stay in the program. At a minimum, CAMP schools usually require that students maintain a B average, keeping up their grades at both the arts school and home school (Rafferty, 2004).

The six CAMP model schools include: The Greater Hartford Academy of the Arts (The Academy; Hartford, CT), The Educational Center for the Arts (ECA; New Haven, CT), The Fine Arts Center (FAC; Greenville, SC), The Governor's School for the Arts (GSA; Norfolk, VA), New Orleans Center for the Creative Arts-Riverfront (NOCCA/Riverfront; New Orleans, LA), and Youth Performing Arts School (YPAS; Louisville, KY). All are located in metropolitan areas east of the Mississippi river. Most of them serve between 200 and 500 students annually. The schools offer both honors credit and regular courses toward high school graduation and Advanced Placement (AP) courses such as AP Visual Art Studio, AP Visual Art Portfolio, and AP Music Theory (R. S. Fluhrer, personal communication, March 16, 2006). Honors-weighted credits are worth more than regular class credits (an "A" in a regular class translates to 4 points, but to 5 points for an honors class). Classes may count toward states' high school graduation requirements in the areas of physical education, social studies, and the arts. Students spend between 12 and 15 intensive hours per week pursuing artistic excellence under the guidance of practicing arts professionals and educators. Those in productions and exhibitions spend additional time in rehearsals and in preparation outside of the normal school hours. The schools also host college, university, and conservatory representatives, who audition students for placement in their performing arts programs. These offerings allow students the opportunity to audition for educational and professional programs and to receive special scholarships. Additional information on the six CAMP model schools can be found in Table 1, with each school' contact information detailed in Appendix B.

Seen as a group, Cluster Arts Magnet Programs include students with diverse cultural backgrounds, experiences, and interests in the arts. The classes may be individual lessons, small or large groups, or rehearsals. The specialized coursework provides for a balance of training in technical skills and in imaginative

Table 1

Description of Cluster Arts Magnet Programs

Cluster Arts Magnet Programs and Arts Domains Served	Year Established and Location	Grades Served	Enrollment	Admissions Criteria	Typical Schedule	Notes
Educational Center for the Arts CW, D, I, MT, T, VA	New Haven, CT	9–12	253	Student auditions are considered for placement only; entrance is by lottery.	1–4 p.m., Monday through Thursday	
New Orleans Center for Creative Arts CW, D, F, I, MT, T, TT, VA, VO	New Orleans, LA	9–12	320	Audition.	Afternoon, late day, Saturday, and summer attendance is offered.	
The Fine Arts Center CW, D, F, I, T, VA	1974 Greenville, SC	9–12	250	Selection is based on talent, interest, motivation and commitment to their discipline.	110 minutes of instruction in the morning or afternoon, Monday through Friday.	
Youth Performing Arts School D, I, TT, VO	1977 Louisville, KY	9–12		Audition.	2-hour blocks are integrated into the high school schedule.	All students take their academic classes at DuPont Manual High School.
Academy of the Arts CW, D, I, MT, T, TT, VA, VO	1985 Hartford, CT	9–12	400	Student auditions are considered for placement only; entrance is by lottery.	Three periods of classes from 1–4:15 p.m., Monday through Thursday.	All students must re-audition each year to maintain admission.
The Governors School for the Arts D, I, MT, T, VA, VO	1987 Norfolk, VA	9–12	345	Audition.	3-hour blocks, Monday through Friday.	

Note. CW = creative writing, D = dance, F = film and video production, I = instrumental music, MT = musical theatre, T = theatre, TT = technical theatre, VA = visual art, VO = vocal music.

and creative skills. Classroom experiences encourage students to develop an understanding of how their art form relates to other art forms. In addition, students receive career and college information and guidance.

Elementary Arts Magnet Schools

In contrast to programs at the secondary level that may provide domain-specific programs, almost all elementary arts magnet schools attribute their innovative academic programs to the way they relate the arts to other school subjects (Daniel, 2000; Wilson, 2001). Although integration of arts into all areas of instruction characterizes most elementary arts magnet programs, there is some variation to the delivery of instruction. Some schools utilize multiaged classroom teams for arts integration (Gratto, 2002), and most programs necessitate that the arts specialist have common planning time with classroom teachers (Gratto, 2002). Besides integration, arts magnet schools also are characterized by enrichment and acceleration. Enrichment means that children are exposed to a wider variety of art forms than the typical elementary school program (Gratto, 2002). An example of acceleration in an elementary art magnet program is when students elect one arts domain in which to concentrate and spend part of the school day studying it.

Learning and assessment are more active and authentic in the elementary arts school setting. "Seat work" is less frequent and more of the senses are engaged (Elliot, 1999). The public also assesses the achievements of students attending arts magnet schools when work is presented and judged by visitors and critics through concerts, competitions, dance recitals, theatrical productions, films, videos, and exhibitions of paintings, photography, and sculpture (Daniel, 2000). In art magnets, active learning also means that continuous assessment methods, such as process portfolios, are used (Clark & Zimmerman, 1998; Wilson, 2001).

Daniel (2000) stated that, "when the arts pervade a school . . . they transform institutional places into attractive, warm, welcoming, and visually exciting places" (p. 382). Arts integration activities tend to sprout dioramas, centers, and sculpted spaces. Teachers, students, and parents in arts magnet schools often see themselves as members of communities that extend beyond the school walls (Elliot, 1999; Wilson, 2001). When students of the arts, their parents, and teachers do things together outside of the regular school day, they feel they have a role in creating and maintaining the community (Wilson, 2001). The school community is widened further with artist-in-residence programs and field trips to local museums, theatres, and galleries.

Even in the current climate of high-stakes assessment and standards-based learning, integrating the arts at the elementary level seems to be less threatening to parents concerned with college entrance and career preparation (Daniel, 2000). In fact, elementary arts magnet schools are characterized by parental involvement (Elliot, 1999). Even when parents are not personally involved in music or art, Freeman (2000) found that artistically talented children come from families who give them encouragement and extra financial support. Freeman also reported that a supportive home environment for the child developing art talent includes displaying both the child's paintings and the artwork of other family members, as well as strong use of color and concern for home décor and arrangement. Appendix C provides contact information and profiles of selected elementary arts magnet schools.

State-Supported, Residential Art Schools

Currently, there are six state-supported, residential high schools that serve the academic, artistic, and creative needs of talented high-achieving students in the United States. Although there are many other high schools and private schools for the arts, these are the only schools that provide tuition-free residential programs. The North Carolina School of the Arts (NCSA), established in 1963, was the first state-supported, residential school of its kind in the nation. The Alabama School of Fine

Arts (ASFA) received legislative approval in 1971, followed by the South Carolina Governor's School for the Arts and Humanities (SCGSAH) in 1980; the Louisiana School for Math, Science, and the Arts (LSMSA) in 1982; the Perpich Center for Arts Education (PCAE) in Minnesota in 1985; and, most recently, the Mississippi School of the Arts (MSA) in 1999. Contact information for the schools can be found in Appendix D.

Infrastructure. The demands for the residential facilities serving artistically talented students are unique. In addition to traditional classroom spaces, facilities must include studios, theatres, labs, student housing, and areas for dining and activities. Residential schools sometimes require newly constructed buildings, as well as the renovation of "found" structures originally built for other purposes.

Some residential schools are located on college campuses. For example, the Louisiana School for Math, Science, and the Arts is located on the campus of Northwestern Louisiana University, yet it has its own residence halls, a student activity center, a restored historic high school building, and annex used for classrooms, labs, and studios.

The North Carolina School of the Arts is a freestanding campus within the University of North Carolina system and is accredited to award the high school diploma, the College Arts Diploma, the Professional Artist Certificate, and bachelor's and master's degrees. The campus consists of a cluster of conservatories serving its full academic program. Included are residence halls and classrooms just for the high school students who make use of a renovated high school, as well as other downtown buildings in Winston-Salem.

The Alabama School of Fine Arts boasts a new instructional and performance complex in downtown Birmingham. Similarly, the South Carolina Governor's School for the Arts and Humanities built a new campus on 8.5 acres on the banks of the Reedy River in Greenville in 1999. Both the Perpich Center for Arts Education and the Mississippi School of the Arts utilize the campuses of former junior colleges. MSA students take some of their nonarts courses (math, science, and foreign languages) at Brookhaven High School, located approximately one half mile from the arts campus.

Admissions. Similar to other schools that provided preprofessional training in the visual and performing arts, most residential schools use transcripts, teacher recommendations, and essays as a screening process, inviting a selection of promising students for an onsite audition. Depending on the discipline, the audition may consist of a portfolio evaluation, a rehearsed monologue, a still-life drawing assignment, or a personal interview with the student. For the residential school, the personal interview may take on more significance because of the level of maturity that is required for a prospective high school student to live and attend school away from friends and family.

Curriculum. Rigorous academic and specialized art curricula characterize most residential programs providing both enrichment and acceleration (Clark & Zimmerman, 2004). The arts curriculum of residential schools extends beyond the traditional school disciplines of music and visual arts to include dance, theatre, theatrical design and production, communication arts, creative writing, museum studies, or film production. A wide variety of performance options may be offered such as ethnic dance, African drumming, chamber music, vocal jazz, or steel pan music (Gratto, 2002). The arts may be taught mainly through performance, in general classroom settings, or in a combination of both (Gratto, 2002).

There are many different ways in which these programs help students integrate and synthesize knowledge from several content areas (Passow, 1992). Most of the residential schools encourage students studying in one arts discipline to take elective courses in other arts areas. For example, the choral group at the Perpich Center for Arts Education is made up of students from all arts areas, not just those studying vocal music (Gratto, 2002).

Another interdisciplinary model often used in residential schools uses themes to cut across several fields. Interdisciplinary studies like architecture or "Making Music with Clay" utilize topics in one area that contribute to another (Gratto, 2002). Abraham Tannenbaum's curriculum model outlined in Passow (1992) suggests four rings consisting of training in specific fields, interdisciplinary studies, community involvement, and humanistic values. Many of the residential schools for the arts also incorporate a community service component into the curriculum. Also, as a form of interdisciplinary enrichment, the schools host guest authors, artists, and performers. A program called the "Common Experience" at the Perpich Center for Art Education brings in a visiting artist from a different discipline every 2 weeks to meet with all students in the school (Gratto, 2002).

Both the South Carolina Governor's School for the Arts and Humanities and the North Carolina School of the Arts build on a master/apprentice model. In this model, students study with resident master teachers who have had successful careers in the arts and who remain active in their professions. In this vein, the North Carolina School of the Arts gets noteworthy attention for its ability to bring in distinguished artists and those accomplished both on stage and screen. The students and faculty present more than 400 public performances and screenings annually in the school's facilities in Winston-Salem, as well as across the state and the Southeast, in major U.S. cities, and overseas.

Personnel. Traditionally, public schools hire certified arts educators to provide arts instruction. Residential schools, and some magnet schools for the artistically talented, follow different guidelines for art teacher staffing to meet the needs of their students. Artistically talented students need teachers with somewhat different characteristics who use different social and educational strategies than teachers of academically gifted students (Clark & Zimmerman, 2002; Gratto, 2002). The specific subject matter expertise requires that teachers are practicing artists who have a desire and the ability to share their art form with students. Where local legislation permits, professionally experienced and active artists/teachers are part of the faculty. Arts schools utilize both certified teachers and artists/teachers who do not hold traditional teacher certification (Daniel, 2000; Gratto, 2002).

Private Institutions

Given limited state funds and a limit to the number of students that district- and state-supported schools can educate, some parents choose to explore the option of private art schools. Although the cost of private schools is prohibitive for some, there are reasons why other families prefer to send their child to a private school. In several communities across the United States, parochial education is the norm. Within a family, parents and grandparents may have a history of going to a particular private school. In other words, some parents prefer private education. Other parents believe that private programs enroll an elite clientele that will benefit their child in his or her arts career. Parents are particularly motivated to seek private institutions when public programs are not available or when private schools have longer hours, better facilities, or a residential component. Several of the country's renowned schools are included in the private school directory in Appendix E.

Private Instruction and Mentorship

For young artists, much of their talent development depends upon their interactions with adult artists. Because the feudal system of apprenticeship no longer exists, young artists need their parents to help them find these resources. Some of the same schools and residential programs profiled here also offer afterschool and summer programs.

Local artists, art guilds, and community art centers also may provide afterschool enrichment courses, extended art activities, and opportunities to explore new media. Yet, many professional artists who do not offer formal instruction may be interested in mentoring young students who are interested in the arts. The opportunity for a service project to assist an artist in putting up an exhibition or preparing supplies could potentially teach the young artist much more, than for example, spending a quiet afternoon in a watercolor class. Opportunities to meet local artists are likely when the local art guild or community art center has an open house, art exhibit, art sale, studio tour, or art classes open to mixed ages. Making sure that a young artist has opportunities to exhibit artwork also is an important part of supporting his or her growth. By involving the child in the selection, preparation, and exhibition of artwork, he or she will have the opportunity to build upon higher order thinking skills involved in aesthetics and art criticism. Furthermore, interaction with an adult artist has the potential to provide an adolescent with the kind of authentic guidance that a parent or teacher cannot provide.

Curricula for the visual and performing arts tends not to be standardized, however a structured program must be designed to encourage consistent work patterns and the skills necessary to confront frustration (Clark & Zimmerman, 2001). A comprehensive program for artistically talented students must be based upon a sequential, articulated curriculum (Clark & Zimmerman, 2002). In *Teaching Talented Art Students* (2004), Gilbert Clark and Enid Zimmerman provide a program structure for a general visual art curriculum that accommodates various levels of achievement and relates the instruction to the understanding of works of artists, art historians, art critics, and aestheticians. The authors' theoretical framework for educating talented students is formulated through the integration of Discipline-Based Art Education and the application of D. H. Feldman's (1985) "Universal to Unique Continuum" theory of art talent development. Each developmental domain in the curriculum model is seen as a level of achievement within specific bodies of knowledge. The developmental domains are ordered from Introductory, to Rudimentary, to Intermediate, to Advanced, to Mastery Stages. Appropriate content for each learner's stage is explored across four strands: Art Making, Art Criticism, Art History, and Aesthetics. The assumption is that students begin their studies of visual art at a naïve stage and as a result of planned teacher interventions and activities, exit at a more sophisticated level. For example, at the introductory stage, learners begin the Art Criticism strand by acquiring basic vocabulary. At each progressive stage, students learn to use that vocabulary in order to categorize works of art through description and analysis. At any place on the structure, artistically talented students would be enriched by reaching greater depth of knowledge, skills, and values than that achieved by most students. Figure 2 offers some suggestions to assist teachers, parents, and students in reaching those greater goals.

Discipline-Based Art Education

Discipline-Based Art Education (DBAE) is a curricular approach found in high-quality art educational settings such as residential arts schools and other public art school programs. The discipline-based goals use a processing skills orientation to select content from the professional fields of art history, art criticism, art production, and aesthetics. Thus, a comprehensive program for artistically talented students is based upon a sequential and articulated curriculum. DBAE is a form of inquiry-based training; the focus is on the students and their interests, judgment, reasoning, and critical thinking skills. Group discussions and problem solving play significant roles in the curriculum, and classroom teachers are viewed as important collaborators in the process. Dobbs (1998) outlined the four strands of Discipline-Based Art Education as:

1. *Art Production*—Students learn skills and techniques in order to produce personal, original artwork.
2. *Art History*—Students study the artistic accomplishments of the past and present as motivation; examples of style or technique; and as discussion topics, especially in relation to

Teacher Strategies

No matter the setting in which teachers encounter artistically talented students, they need to develop specific, written curriculum plans. Plans may differ in terms of emphasis, detail, artwork, and activities, but Dobbs (1998) made it clear that teachers should include in their curriculum:

- a long-range plan and written lessons that ensure that curricular activities are specific, well understood, and coordinated with other grades or levels;
- sequential organization that allows skills and concepts to build on one another;
- engagement with works of art by mature artists from many cultures;
- content that is balanced among the four art disciplines (production, history, criticism, and aesthetics); and
- developmentally suitable and age-appropriate learning activities.

Parent Strategies

- Provide children with art materials and art books of their own.
- Provide places where children can study their arts discipline, practice their work, and display or perform.
- Participate in some of your children's arts activities.
- Let children learn about and share in some of your artistic interests.
- Take children on trips to points of artistic interest.
- Enable children to take advantage of lessons and activities offered by private groups or community organizations.

Student Strategies

- Practice, practice, practice!
- Record and save work in a portfolio.
- Evaluate yourself and rate your own performance on the pieces that you choose to keep for your portfolio. Be honest with yourself. Learn to separate your sentimental feelings about your work from realistic judgments of quality.
- If you do not have the resources in your school or community to help develop your talent, join with other students to form an arts club. Sample goals for the club could be to raise money for a field trip to a museum or concert or to bring a resident artist to your school.

Figure 2. Practical strategies for developing skills in the arts.

cultural, political, social, religious, and economic events and movements.

3. *Art Criticism*—Students describe, interpret, evaluate, theorize, and judge the properties and qualities of the visual form, for the purpose of understanding and appreciating works of art and understanding the roles of art in society.

4. *Aesthetics*—Students consider the nature, meaning, impact, and value of art; are encouraged to formulate reflective, "educated" opinions and judgments about specific works of art; and examine criteria for evaluating works of art.

Special Issues and the Artistically Talented Student

The next step in supporting artistically talented children is to help them build self-confidence in their own creative abilities and intelligence. Unlike young mathematicians or scientists, the achievements of young artists are not seen in the public eye or in the field of education as reflective of intellectual ability (Clark & Zimmerman, 1998). Talent development, when it refers to high ability in the arts, is treated differently from talent development in gifted and talented literature because so few researchers and educators have studied high ability in the arts, and there is little agreement about what constitutes talent, what it looks like, and how it should be defined (Clark & Zimmerman, 1998; Zimmerman, 2004). Young visual artists usually are recognized for outstanding skills in drawing, yet they also may excel because they demonstrate original ideas or innovations independent of advanced skills. Other indicators of talent in the arts may be high levels of motivation, passion, perseverance, or problem-solving skills (Clark & Zimmerman, 1998). When young artists excel, it is evident that they are drawing upon diverse sources of human abilities including aspirations, aesthetics, perception, sensitivity, and the capacity for reflection (Golomb, 2002).

Identification

Although a conservative estimate of the population of intellectually gifted students in the United States may be 2%–5%, this can't be seen as a limit (Gallagher, 2003). There should exist a similar number of artistically talented students, whether formally identified or not. Clark and Zimmerman (2004) promoted an expanded perspective on the distribution of art talent in the population. Using Clark's Drawing Abilities Test (CDAT), a standardized instrument used to measure visual art abilities, the authors established that like intelligence, art talent is normally distributed in a pattern similar to the Bell Curve. Therefore, according to these authors, almost everyone is endowed with at least some aptitude for talent development in the arts. There are a few students with superior artistic abilities, but most have abilities somewhere in the average range.

Furthermore, those who are identified as intellectually gifted do not preclude those who also are young artists, musicians, actors, dancers, or creative writers. Sternberg and Lubart (1993) have argued that people of high mental ability are predisposed to creative acts when other characteristics also are present. Unfortunately, such characteristics like tolerance of ambiguity, moderate risk taking, perseverance, openness to new ideas, and substantial self-concept often go unsupported in gifted and regular school programs (Gallagher, 2003).

Recognition and respect of a wide range of abilities and talents in the classroom is of utmost importance. Teachers should go out of their way to engage students in cooperative tasks that demand different abilities and talents from different students. In this regard, the multiple intelligences perspective may help artistically talented students appreciate their own strengths and weaknesses, as well as those of others. Teachers of the artistically talented should identify transferable skills and abilities as a part of their instructional activities. Encouraging artistically talented adolescents to explore many career options may help them see the relevance of schooling, and an interest in a career path may help maintain enough academic involvement and achievement to mitigate low self-concept in an academic area.

Stereotypes

Young artists may have to deal with several cultural stereotypes that are based on both fact and fiction. Because art historians and art educators often have emphasized the peculiar characteristics of successful artists, the stereotype exists equating artistic genius with mental illness (Rush, 1997). The notion that craziness is an important aspect of being an artist and that it makes one a better artist may affect young artists. This myth of the eccentric genius is responsible for much of the public ambivalence about art and artists and can have a negative effect on talent development (Rush, 1997).

American culture also has negative stereotypes about male dancers, and has yet to accept minority artists in prime acting and dancing roles (Perez, 2005; Williams, 2003). Noting the true lack of funding for art programs, and a limited future for possible earning potential of artists, parents may not wish their child to pursue a career in the arts for fear of them becoming a "starving artist." Yet, according to 2006–2007 U.S. Department of Labor statistics, more people are employed in the visual arts than in all of the performing arts and sports industries combined. Figure 3 offers a range of practical strategies to support the affective needs of young visual and performing artists.

When stereotypes about artists are negative and inaccurate, the potential for damaging individuals is all the greater. Perhaps equally damaging, stereotypes also may become self-fulfilling prophecies, especially for young artists. Having internalized the stereotypes, they may think, for example, that to be an artist they must suppress their talents in other academic areas. The existence of an atmosphere that socially discourages achievement in the arts or pursuing a career in the arts may have a substantial impact on the way that artistically talented students view themselves (Shavinina & Ferrari, 2004).

Teacher Strategies
- Encourage inquiry and openness to new ideas in the classroom.
- Identify transferable skills and abilities as a part of the instructional activities.
- Be tolerant of ambiguity.
- Encourage moderate risk taking.
- Encourage perseverance.
- Substantiate self-concept.
- Encourage artistically talented adolescents to explore many career options to help them see the relevance of schooling.

Parent Strategies
- Avoid comparing children with one another.
- Show children that they are loved for their own sake and not merely for artistic achievements.
- Try to find something specific to praise when children show you their work or when you listen or watch their performance. A generalized compliment means little to any child.

Student Strategies

- Remind yourself that it takes time for an artist to develop his or her own style. While you are growing up, it is tempting to compare yourself to mature artists and to artistic peers. With time, you will eventually master the fundamentals of your artistic domain, and only then can your own style emerge.
- Keep track of your feelings in a journal and reflect on how your self-confidence in your art changes over time. This is especially important when you have a special opportunity to develop your talent. Keep a log of how you feel before, during, and after a big recital, art opening, or poetry reading.
- Make sure to tell the people who are closest to you how you feel about making your art. They may not be able to perceive your sensitivities or realize your needs unless you express how you really feel.

Figure 3. Practical strategies for supporting the affective needs of young artists.

Conclusion

When children study the arts, they learn to observe, envision, and reflect upon their working process. In the process of creating, artists visualize and set goals to find and define a problem, choose techniques to collect data, reflect on their work, consider alternative points of view, evaluate and revise the problem's solution, try out changes, and begin the cycle of revision again. Comparing this process to the scientific method makes a convincing argument for art as a critical and complex experience. In order to provide both enrichment and acceleration for the artistically talented child, rigorous academic and specialized art programming are necessary. Therefore, the attitudes described here really are very similar for parents and teachers of an artistic child and those of an intellectually gifted child.

Four steps for supporting talent in the visual and performing arts are emphasized:

1. raise levels of arts awareness;
2. understand the purpose of art in our society;
3. find special opportunities to observe, create, reflect, and learn; and
4. build self-confidence of creative abilities and intelligence.

Without these steps, there is little hope for developing the potential and promise of our nation's most talented students.

Web Sites

American Society for Aesthetics
http://www.aesthetics-online.org

The official Web site of the American Society for Aesthetics and teaching resource for philosophy of art, art theory, and art criticism.

ArtLex.com
http://www.artlex.com

An online dictionary of art terms including supporting images, pronunciation notes, quotations, and crossreferences.

ArtsEdge—National Arts and Education Network
http://artsedge.kennedy-center.org

A free, standards-based lesson plan archive that also includes professional development resources, student materials, and guidelines for arts instruction and assessment.

Educational Theatre Association (EdTA)
http://www.edta.org

The official Web site of EdTA, the professional organization for theatre education.

International NETWORK of Schools for the Advancement of Arts Education
http://www.artsschoolsnetwork.org

A professional development organization for schools, instructional programs, and postsecondary institutions of the arts.

The Metropolitan Museum of Art
http://www.metmuseum.org

The official Web site of the Metropolitan Museum of Art. It includes teacher resources, an interactive gallery, and a searchable database.

MENC: The National Association for Music Education
http://www.menc.org

The official Web site of MENC, the professional organization for music education.

National Art Education Association (NAEA)
http://www.naea-reston.org

The official Web site of NAEA, the professional organization for art education.

Witcombe's Art History Resources on the Web
http://witcombe.sbc.edu/ARTHLinks.html

A comprehensive list of Web resources for world art history, from ancient to contemporary.

Words of Art
http://web.ubc.ca/okanagan/creative/links/glossary.html

An online glossary of theory and criticism for the visual arts.

World Wide Arts Resources Corporation
http://wwar.com

A gateway for contemporary visual and performing arts news, art blogs, art history, contemporary artists, and gallery portfolios.

References

Baton Rouge Center for Visual and Performing Arts. (n.d.). *Home page.* Retrieved April 26, 2007, from http://brcvpa. ebrschools.org/explore.cfm/aboutourschool

Bloom, B. S. (1985). *Developing talent in young people.* New York: Ballantine.

Bureau of Labor Statistics, U.S. Department of Labor. (n.d.). *Occupational outlook handbook, 2006–07 edition: Artists and related workers.* Retrieved October 13, 2007, from http:// www.bls.gov/oco/ocos092.htm

Clark, G., & Zimmerman, E. (1998). Nurturing the arts in programs for gifted and talented students. *Phi Delta Kappan, 79,* 747–751.

Clark, G., & Zimmerman, E. (2002). Tending the special spark: Accelerated and enriched curricula for highly talented art students. *Roeper Review, 24,* 161–168.

Clark, G., & Zimmerman, E. (2004). *Teaching talented art students: Principles and practices.* New York: Teachers College.

Coleman, L. J. (2002). A shock to study. *Journal of Secondary Gifted Education, 14,* 39–52.

Csikszentmihalyi, M., Rathunde, K., & Whalen, S. (1993). *Talented teenagers: The roots of success and failure.* New York: Cambridge University.

Daniel, R. (2000). Performing and visual arts schools: A guide to characteristics, options, and successes. *Journal of Secondary Gifted Education, 12,* 43–48.

Dobbs, S. M. (1998). *Learning in and through art: A guide to discipline-based art education.* Los Angeles: J. Paul Getty Trust.

Elliot, I. (1999, October). Learning through the arts. *Teaching PreK–8, 30,* 38–41.

Ericsson, K. A., Krampe, R. T., & Tesch-Romer, C. (1993). The role of deliberate practice in the acquisition of expert performance. *Psychological Review, 100,* 363–406.

Feldman, D. H. (1985). The concept of non-universal developmental domains: Implications for artistic development. *Visual Arts Research, 11,* 82–89.

Feldman, D. H. (1999). The development of creativity. In R. J. Sternberg (Ed.), *Handbook of creativity* (pp. 169–183). New York: Cambridge University.

Freeman, J. (2000). Children's talent in fine art and music. *Roeper Review, 22,* 98–101.

Gagné, F. (2003). Transforming gifts into talents: The DMGT as a developmental theory. In N. Colangelo & G. A. Davis (Eds.), *Handbook of gifted education* (pp. 60–74). Boston: Allyn & Bacon.

Gallagher, J. J. (2003). Issues and challenges in the education of gifted students. In N. Colangelo & G. A. Davis (Eds.), *Handbook of gifted education* (pp. 11–23). Boston: Allyn & Bacon.

Garrick, M. B. (2005). The dance spirit performing arts high school guide 2005. *Dance Spirit, 9*(3), 94–107.

Getzels, J. B., & Csikszentmihalyi, M. (1976). *The creative vision.* New York: Wiley.

Golomb, C. (1995). *The development of artistically gifted children: Selected case studies.* Hillsdale, NJ: Lawrence Erlbaum.

Golomb, C. (2002). *Child art in context: A cultural and comparative perspective.* Washington, DC: American Psychological Association.

Gratto, S. D. (2002). Arts education in alternative school formats. *Arts Education Policy Review, 103*(5), 17–26.

Gray, K. M., & Kunkel, M. A. (2001). The experience of female ballet dancers: A grounded theory. *High Ability Studies, 12*(1), 7–25.

Haroutounian, J. (1995). Talent identification and development in the arts: An artistic/educational dialogue. *Roeper Review, 18,* 112–117.

International NETWORK of Schools for the Advancement of Arts Education. (n.d.). *Home page.* Retrieved March 8, 2006, from http://www.artsschoolsnetwork.org

Izawa-Hayden, A. (2002). *The art of learning.* Retrieved March 8, 2007, from http://www.connectforkids.org/node/421

Jacob K. Javits Gifted and Talented Students Education Act of 1988, Pub. L. No. 100-297, Title IV, Part B, §4101 et seq. (1988).

Mickelson, A. (2003). Dance h.s. *Dance Spirit, 7*(3), 66–69.

Milbrath, C. (1998). *Patterns of artistic development in children: Comparative studies of talent.* New York: Cambridge University.

National Association for Gifted Children. (2005a). *Arts division.* Retrieved June 14, 2007, from http://www.nagc.org/index.aspx?id=1415

National Association for Gifted Children. (2005b). *What is gifted?* Retrieved June 14, 2007, from http://www.nagc.org/index.aspx?id=574&an

Passow, A. H. (1992, January/February). A residential high school for gifted in arts and science. *Gifted Child Today, 15,* 2–7.

Perez, G. (2005). A moving force: In the country's biggest minority, Latino artists fight stereotypes that blur their artistry and their diversity. *Dance Magazine, 79,* 52–55.

Piirto, J. (1992). *Understanding those who create.* Dayton, OH: Ohio Psychology Press.

Rafferty, H. R. (2004). All jazzed up. *Stage Directions, 17*(5), 50–51.

Rossell, C. (2005). Magnet schools. *Education Next, 4*(2), 44–49.

Rostan, S. M. (2003). In the spirit of Howard E. Gruber's gift: Case studies of two young artists' evolving systems. *Creativity Research Journal, 15*(1), 45–60.

Rush, J .C. (1997). The myth of the eccentric genius: Some thoughts on political correctness and art education. *Arts Education Policy Review, 97*, 1063–2913.

Shavinina, L. V., & Ferrari, M. (2004). Extracognitive facets of developing high ability: Introduction to some important issues. In L. V. Shavinina & M. Ferrari (Eds.), *Beyond knowledge: Extracognitive aspects of developing high ability* (pp. 3–13). Mahwah, NJ: Laurence Erlbaum.

Shuter-Dyson, R. (1985). Musical giftedness. In J. Freeman (Ed.), *The psychology of gifted children* (pp. 159–183). New York: Wiley.

Sloboda, J. (1996). The acquisition of musical performance expertise: Deconstructing the "talent" account of individual differences in musical expressivity. In K. A. Ericsson (Ed.), *The road to excellence: The acquisition of expert performance in the arts and sciences, sports, and games* (pp. 107–126). Hillsdale, NJ: Lawrence Erlbaum.

Sosniak, L. (1985). One concert pianist. In B. Bloom (Ed.), *Developing talent in young people* (pp. 68–89). New York: Ballantine.

Sternberg R. J., & Lubart, T. I. (1993). Creative giftedness: A multivariate investment approach. *Gifted Child Quarterly, 37*, 7–15.

Tannenbaum, A. J. (2003). Nature and nurture of giftedness. In N. Colangelo & G. A. Davis (Eds.), *Handbook of gifted education* (pp. 45–59). Boston: Allyn & Bacon.

Williams, D. (2003). Examining psychosocial issues of adolescent male dancers. (Doctoral dissertation, Marywood University,

2003). *Dissertation Abstracts International, 64*, 5A. (UMI No. 3090242)

Wilson, B. (2001). Arts magnets and the transformation of schools and schooling. *Education & Urban Society, 33*, 366–387.

Winner, E. (1996). *Gifted children: Myths and realities.* New York: Basic.

Winner, E., & Hetland, L. (Eds.). (2000, Fall/Winter). The arts and academic achievement: What the evidence shows. *Journal of Aesthetic Education, 34*(3–4).

Zimmerman, E. (2004). *Artistically and musically talented students: Essential readings in gifted education.* Thousand Oaks, CA: Corwin Press.

Appendix A
List of Characteristics of Artistic Children

- Aware of their talents
- Have a concern for developing technical skills
- Introspective about the role of the arts in their lives
- Find making art rewarding
- Break from tradition
- Demonstrate autonomy, independence, and flexibility
- Show sensitivity to their environment and to others
- Prefer more complexity to simplicity
- Desire education in their domain
- Not shy about showing emotions
- Impulsive in behavior
- Able to delay closure in judgments about morality, politics, and social phenomena
- "Experimenters with the new"
- Prefer more ambiguity to emphasis on the right answer
- More androgynous
- Able to name a favorite artist

Appendix B
Directory of Cluster Arts Magnet Programs

ACES Educational Center for the Arts
55 Audubon Street
New Haven, CT 06510
(203) 777-5451
http://www.aces.k12.ct.us/schools/eca

The Fine Arts Center
102 Pine Knoll Drive
Greenville, SC 29609
(864) 355-2551
http://www.fineartscenter.net

Governor's School for the Arts
c/o Old Dominion University
Norfolk, VA 23529
(757) 451-4711
http://www.gsarts.net

Greater Hartford Academy of the Arts
15 Vernon Street
Hartford, CT 06106
(860) 757-6300
http://www.crec.org/magnetschools/schools/artsacademy

New Orleans Center for Creative Arts
2800 Chartres Street
New Orleans, LA 70117
(800) 201-4836
http://www.nocca.com

Youth Performing Arts School
1517 South Second Street
Louisville, KY 40208
(502) 485-8355
http://www.jefferson.k12.ky.us/schools/special/YPAS

Appendix C
Selected Elementary Arts Magnet Schools

Baton Rouge Center for Visual and Performing Arts
2040 South Acadian Thruway
Baton Rouge, LA 70808
(225) 344-0084
http://brcvpa.ebrschools.org/explore.cfm/aboutourschool

The Baton Rouge Center for Visual and Performing Arts (BRCVPA) is a K–5 elementary magnet school, serving approximately 400 students from East Baton Rouge Parish in Louisiana. The program is characterized by arts enrichment and arts integration. BRCVPA has been nationally recognized by the Kennedy Center Alliance for Arts Education Network and the Louisiana Alliance for Arts Education (as a Creative Ticket-School of Excellence) for its achievements in arts education.

Berkeley Arts Magnet at the Whittier School
1645 Milvia St.
Berkeley, CA 94709
(510) 644-6225
http://www.bampta.org

Berkeley Arts Magnet at the Whittier School was a California Distinguished School in 1989, 1993, 1997, and 2000. The school is characterized by its "Artist Time" program. In the lower grades, students are exposed to choral music, percussion, African dance, visual art, and drama on a weekly basis. In the upper grades, children elect one area in which to concentrate, and spend one hour four afternoons a week studying their chosen form. The program is designed to expose young students to a wide range of arts experiences while giving older children more advanced training during an elective period.

Bethune Elementary School of the Arts
2400 Meade Street
Hollywood, FL 33020
(754) 323-4900
http://www.broward.k12.fl.us/bethuneelem

Bethune Elementary School of the Arts is a magnet program for the visual and performing arts and draws its students from the south area of Broward County, FL. It provides programs for children from prekindergarten through fifth grade in an extended school day. Students attend classes in two-dimensional art, computer art, three-dimensional art, stagecraft, dance, drama, chorus, band, strings, keyboard, and general music. Students from the primary grades (kindergarten through second grade) take part in an exposure program, rotating through dance, drama, band, keyboard, strings, and the two- and three-dimensional visual arts. Through the program, students begin to discover their areas of strength in the arts and, along with their parents and teachers, are able to make a choice for a major and minor area of focus in grade 3. At the intermediate level (grades 3–5), students pursue intensive training at a more advanced level in the areas they have chosen. At the fifth-grade level, students are prepared for entrance into the middle school performing arts magnet if that is their middle school choice.

Lee Expressive Arts School
1208 Locust Street
Columbia, MO 65201
(573) 214-3530
http://www.columbia.k12.mo.us/Lee

Lee Expressive Arts School is located in downtown Columbia, MO. The school is partnered with Stephens College and the University of Missouri Music and Art Departments. Additionally, visual and performing artists-in-residence are contracted on a yearly basis. The school day is extended in order to provide for the opportunity to explore and experience art, music, movement, drama, literature, and the social and physical sciences through integrated classes.

Thomas G. Pullen K–8 Arts Focus School
700 Bright Seat Road
Landover, MD 20785
(301) 808-8160
http://www.pgcps.pg.k12.md.us/~tpullen

Thomas G. Pullen K–8 Arts Focus School in Prince George's County, MD, is designed to develop the interests and talents of students in the arts and at the same time enhance the academic discipline through an interdisciplinary approach. Classes are taught by specialists in visual art, drama, instrumental and vocal music, dance, creative writing, media production, computer arts, and the literary arts. The school prepares its students for opportunities for specialization in the arts in middle school through enrichment activities after school, opportunities to showcase work created by students, performance opportunities at all levels, visiting artists and guest speakers, field trips, a computer lab for related arts and academic instruction, Suzuki violin or cello lessons for grades K–3, keyboard (piano) lab, music, dance, visual arts, drama and media production facilities, and its Partnerships with the Kennedy Center's CETA (Changing

Education Through the Arts) Program and MATI (Maryland Artist Teacher's Institute).

Appendix D
Directory of State-Supported Residential Schools
for the Arts

Alabama School of Fine Arts
1800 8th Avenue North
Birmingham, AL 35203
(205) 252-9241
http://www.asfa.k12.al.us

Louisiana School for Math, Science, and the Arts
715 University Parkway
Natchitoches, LA 71457
(318) 357-3174
http://www.lsmsa.edu

Mississippi School of the Arts
308 West Cherokee Street
Brookhaven, MS 39601
(601) 823-1300
http://www.msa.k12.ms.us

North Carolina School of the Arts
1533 South Main Street
Winston-Salem, NC 27127
(336) 770-3399
http://www.ncarts.edu

Perpich Center for Arts Education
6125 Olson Memorial Highway
Golden Valley, MN 55422
(763) 591-4700
http://www.pcae.k12.mn.us

South Carolina Governor's School for the Arts and Humanities
15 University Street
Greenville, SC 29601
(864) 282-3777
http://www.scgsah.state.sc.us

Appendix E
Directory of Selected Private Institutions

East Coast

The American Boychoir School
19 Lambert Drive
Princeton, NJ 08540
(609) 924-5858
http://www.americanboychoir.org

Baltimore Actors' Theatre Conservatory
300 Dumbarton Road
Baltimore, MD 21212
(410) 337-8519
http://www.baltimoreactorstheatre.org

The Putney School
418 Houghton Brook Road
Putney, VT 05346
(802) 387-5566
http://www.putneyschool.org

Professional Children's School
132 West 60th Street
New York, NY 10023
(212) 582-3116
http://www.pcs-nyc.org

Saint Thomas Choir School
202 W. 58th Street
New York, NY 10019
(212) 247-3311
http://www.choirschool.org

Walnut Hill School
12 Highland Street
Natick, MA 01760
(508) 653-4312
http://www.walnuthillarts.org

Midwest

The Chicago Academy for the Arts
1010 West Chicago Avenue
Chicago, IL 60622
(312) 421-0202
http://www.chicagoacademyforthearts.org

Interlochen Center for the Arts
P.O. Box 199
Interlochen, MI 49643
(231) 276-7200
http://www.interlochen.org

West Coast

Adda Clevenger Junior Preparatory & Theater School for
Children
180 Fair Oaks
San Francisco, CA 94110
(415) 824-2240
http://www.addaclevenger.org

The Crowden School
1475 Rose Street
Berkeley, CA 94702
(510) 559-6910
http://www.crowden.org

Idyllwild Arts Academy
P.O. Box 38
52500 Temecula Road
Idyllwild, CA 92549
(951) 659-2171
http://www.idyllwildarts.org

Northwest Academy
1130 SW Main Street
Portland, OR 97205
(503) 223-3367
http://www.nwacademy.org

About the Author

Jesse Rachel Cukierkorn is a practicing artist and art educator. She has taught visual art in general and special education settings at the elementary and secondary levels, in both public and private schools in three states. Her teaching experience gave her the inspiration for this text and the foundation for applying both theory and research.

Dr. Cukierkorn has published articles in the *Journal of Cultural Research in Art Education* and *Roeper Review*, and she completed her doctoral degree in gifted education at the University of Southern Mississippi. She resides and works in Miami Beach, FL.

Printed in the United States
by Baker & Taylor Publisher Services